ABCs of FILIPINO CULTURE

A JOURNEY THROUGH THE PHILIPPINES

GUADALUPE RUIZ AND KENDEL BRADY

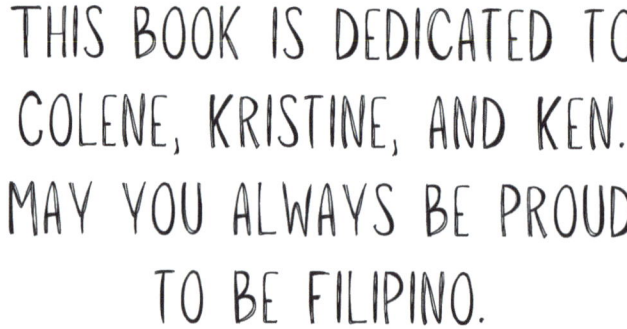

THIS BOOK IS DEDICATED TO COLENE, KRISTINE, AND KEN. MAY YOU ALWAYS BE PROUD TO BE FILIPINO.

Published by Guadalupe Ruiz and Kendel Brady © 2025

No portion of this publication may be reproduced or transmitted in any form or by any means, electronic or mechanical, including, but not limited to, audio recordings, facsimiles, photocopying, or information storage and retrieval systems without explicit written permission from the author or publisher.

Download our Free ABCs of the Philippines Activity Book!

THIS BOOK BELONGS TO

_____

_____

Aa is for **adobo**, a tasty meat stew.

Adobo, a dish with the perfect sweet-salty-sour balance, is a beloved Filipino dish.

Bb is for **bangka**, a Filipino boat.

Fishermen and tourists use bangkas to zoom through the waves, go fishing, and even take a nap in the sun.

Cc is for **carabao**, a strong and gentle animal.

Carabaos are like tractors for farmers. They help plant crops, harvest food, and even give milk!

Dd

is for **duyan**, a hanging basket bed.

Duyan is a traditional Filipino hammock that is often used for sleeping or relaxing.

Ee is for **ensaymada**, a buttery sweet bread.

Ensaymada is a fluffy, buttery pastry that is topped with cheese and sugar.

Ff is for **fiesta**, a village party.

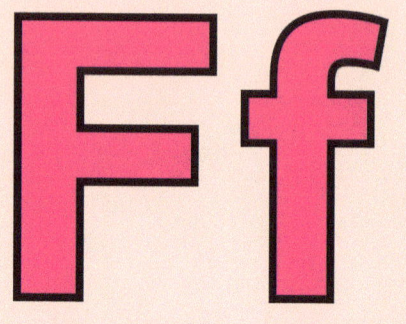

Fiesta is when people come together to eat, dance, and play.

Gg

is for **gulay**, healthy, fresh vegetables.

The Philippines grows a variety of vegetables year-round. People buy gulay from colorful stands around the community.

Hh is for **halo-halo**, a sweet and refreshing treat.

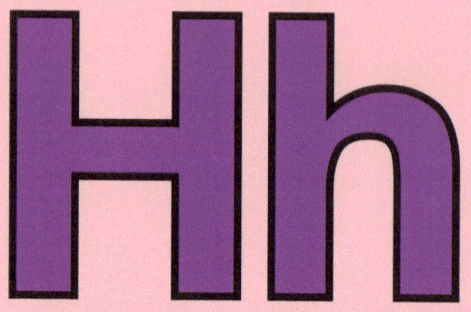

Halo-halo means mix-mix. It is made with shaved ice, milk, and a variety of fruits, jellies, and beans.

Ii

is for **isla**, which means island.

The Philippines is a country made up of more than 7,600 islands!

Jj

is for **jeepney**,
a colorful public
transportation bus.

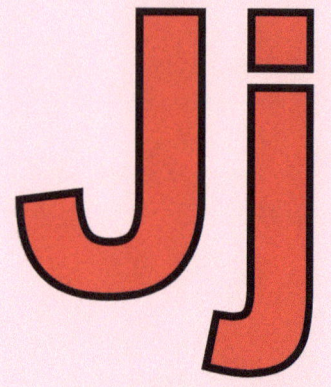

Jeepneys are bright, open-air buses that lots of Filipinos use to go places!

Kk

is for **karaoke**, where we sing and have fun.

Karaoke is a popular way for Filipinos to have fun and bond with friends and family.

Ll

is for **lechon**,
a roasted pig.

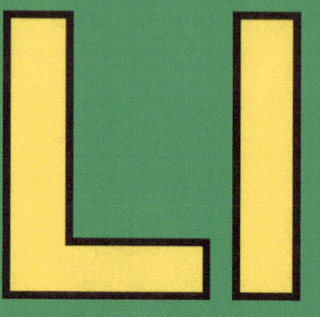

Lechon is often served on special occasions and is known for its crispy skin and juicy meat.

Mm is for **mano**, a blessing from elders.

Mano is a cherished Filipino tradition that shows respect and friendship, where an elder gently places their hand on the younger person's forehead.

Nn is for **nipa**,
a roof made from palm leaves.

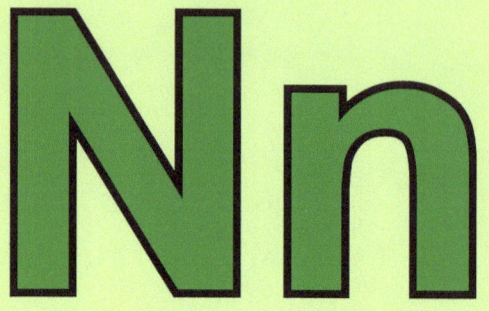

Nipa palm tree leaves are strong and water-resistant, making them ideal for crafting roofs.

Oo is for **OFW**, Overseas Filipino Workers.

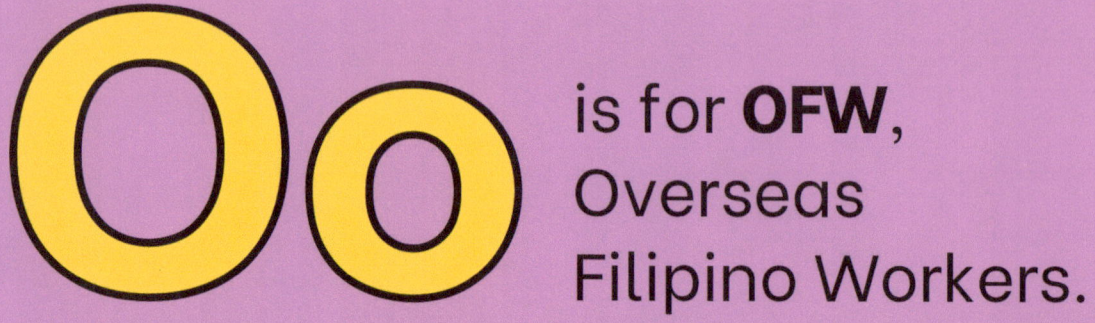

OFWs are Filipinos who go to work in other countries to provide for their families back home.

Pp

is for **pamilya**, which means family.

Filipinos have strong family bonds that extend to grandparents, aunts, uncles, and cousins.

Qq is for **queso de bola**, a ball of cheese.

Queso de bola is a special treat that is a Christmas Eve favorite.

Rr

is for **Rizal**,
the National Hero of
the Philippines.

Jose Rizal was a doctor and writer. He fought for Philippine independence by writing essays and novels which challenged Spanish rule.

Ss is for **sari-sari store**, a neighborhood convenience store.

Sari-sari stores are small, family-owned shops that offer a little bit of everything – from tasty snacks and drinks to household essentials.

Tt

is for **tarsier**, a tiny nocturnal primate.

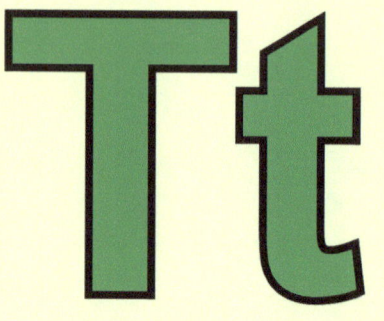

Tarsiers are roughly the size of a human hand. Sadly, they are endangered animals due to habitat loss and hunting.

Uu is for **ube**, a purple root crop.

Ube is native to the Philippines. It has a sweet, nutty flavor, and is often used in desserts.

Vv

is for **volcano**.
There are about 300 volcanoes in the Philippines.

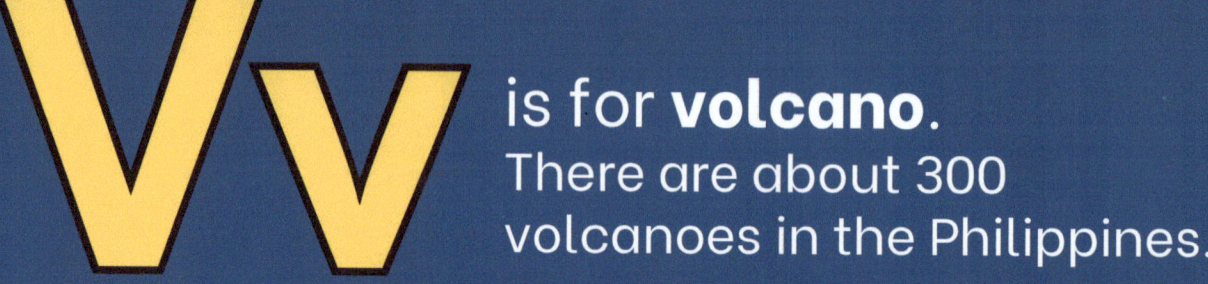

Many Philippine islands were formed by volcanoes. Some are still active like the Mayon Volcano in Bicol.

Ww

is for **walis**, a broom made from grass.

Filipinos use walis, a soft and gentle broom, to sweep away dirt and dust.

Xx is for **extra rice**, because Filipinos love rice!

Rice is grown abundantly across the Philippines. It is a staple in Filipino meals. They say, 'Rice is life' here!

Yy is for **Yaya**, a nanny or caregiver.

Yayas are like extended family members who care for, play with, and teach children.

Zz

is for **zest**
of calamansi,
a small citrus fruit.

Calamansi is a sweet and sour fruit used in Filipino cooking and drinks.

ABOUT THE AUTHORS

Guada is a Filipino writer and special education teacher who grew up in Cebu City, Philippines. She spent her summers in the province, where she developed a love for the traditional Filipino culture and way of life. Guada is passionate about sharing her culture with others.
www.thecleverpinoy.com

Kendel is an American author and educator who currently resides in Bohol, Philippines.
www.kendelbrady.com

Guada and Kendel hope this book will introduce young readers to the beauty and diversity of the Philippines and promote multicultural understanding.

Free Printable Activity Book

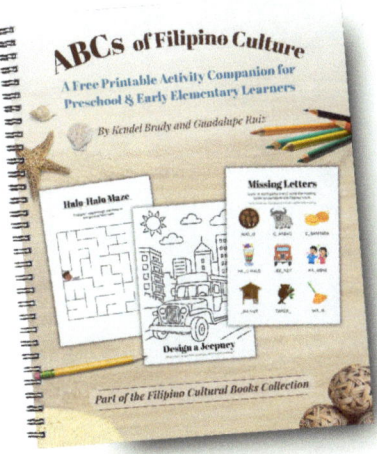

Continue learning! We are delighted to offer complimentary printable activity pages that are designed to enhance the concepts from the story through engaging, hands-on learning.

Download the Free Companion Activities!
www.kendelbrady.com

If your child enjoyed this book, you may also love:

Bahay Kubo: Nipa Hut
A beautifully illustrated picture book based on the beloved Filipino folk song, celebrating plants, food, and connection to the land.

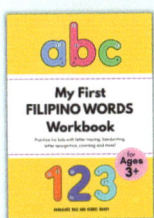

My First Filipino Words Workbook
A hands-on activity book for preschool and kindergarten learners that builds early literacy, handwriting, and number recognition using Filipino cultural vocabulary.

Baybayin Workbook
A beginner-friendly workbook for teens and adults interested in learning the ancient Philippine writing system.

www.ingramcontent.com/pod-product-compliance
Lightning Source LLC
Chambersburg PA
CBHW041945110426
42744CB00027B/19